PERSPECTIVES

DAVID HOWARD

THE SAN FRANCISCO CENTER FOR VISUAL STUDIES

LIBRARY OF CONGRESS CATALOG NUMBER:

77-90787

ISBN 0-930976-00-2

PUBLISHED BY

THE SAN FRANCISCO CENTER FOR VISUAL STUDIES

900 ALABAMA STREET

SAN FRANCISCO, CALIFORNIA

94110

U.S.A.

INTRODUCTION

THE FORMAL ESTABLISHMENT OF PHOTOGRAPHY AS ART BEGAN WHEN DEDICATED ARTISTS IN THE PHOTO-SECESSION MOVEMENT AND IN THE F-64 GROUP REJECTED PICTORIALISM AND PAVED THE WAY FOR THE RECOGNITION OF PHOTOGRAPHY AS AN ART MEDIUM.

INDIVIDUALS IN THESE LOOSELY ORGANIZED GROUPS FOUGHT TOGETHER TO ESTABLISH PHOTOGRAPHY AS A LEGITIMATE ART FORM, THROUGH DISSEMINATION OF PUBLICATIONS, PHOTOGRAPHIC FORUMS AND PERSONALLY SPONSORED EXHIBITIONS.

THE EVOLUTION OF PHOTOGRAPHY IS AN EPISODE IN THE HISTORY OF ART WHICH IS INCOMPLETE. PHOTOGRAPHY AS AN ART FORM HAS BECOME SUCH AN INFLUENTIAL MEDIUM, THAT IT IS BEGINNING TO DOMINATE CONTEMPORARY ART, AND YET, IT STILL HAS NOT REACHED ITS CLIMAX AS AN ART MEDIUM. HOWEVER, BECAUSE PHOTOGRAPHY IS A RELATIVELY YOUNG ART FORM, IT HAS NOT HAD THE ECONOMIC VALUE ATTRIBUTED TO IT THAT THE OTHER ART MEDIUMS HAVE DEVELOPED. THIS HAS HAD MANY RAMIFICATIONS FOR THE PHOTOGRAPHIC ARTISTS OF THE TWENTIETH CENTURY.

A TYPE OF INNOCENCE AND A WILLINGNESS TO BE AVANT-GARDE HAVE DEVELOPED IN THE PERSONALITIES OF SOME OF THE CONTEMPORARY PHOTOGRAPHIC ARTISTS, DUE TO THE FACT THAT THEY CANNOT DIRECTLY PROSPER FROM THE SALE OF THEIR ART WORKS, TO THE EXTENT THAT ARTISTS IN OTHER MEDIUMS DO. AS A RESULT, THEY ARE NOT RELYING ON THEIR PHOTOGRAPHS AS COMMODITIES, BUT EXPERIENCE THEIR PHOTOGRAPHS MORE PURELY FROM AN AESTHETIC STANDPOINT.

THE HISTORY OF PHOTOGRAPHY INDICATES THAT IN THE EARLY PART OF THE TWENTIETH CENTURY, PHOTOGRAPHY WAS AN UNAPPRECIATED ART FORM, EXCEPT FOR A CLOSEKNIT NETWORK OF PEOPLE DEDICATED TO THEIR ART, WHO PRIMARILY SHARED IT ONLY WITH EACH OTHER. NO REAL AUDIENCE FOR PHOTOGRAPHY, AS AN ART FORM, HAD BEEN ESTABLISHED. PHOTOGRAPHIC ENDEAVORS WERE PURELY AESTHETIC PURSUITS, WITH NO ULTERIOR MOTIVES, BECAUSE AN ECONOMIC VENT, OTHER THAN COMMERCIAL PHOTOGRAPHY, WAS UNAVAILABLE. PURCHASING PHOTOGRAPHIC PRINTS FOR COLLECTION PURPOSES WAS UNHEARD OF. AS A RESULT, THERE WERE VERY FEW ECONOMIC OUTLETS,

AND LITTLE, IF ANY, SPONSORED EXHIBITIONS.

PHOTOGRAPHY IS STILL QUESTIONED AS AN ART FORM IN SOME CIRCLES TODAY. THE QUESTIONING IS UNDOUBTEDLY LUDICROUS. PHOTOGRAPHY HAS EVOLVED TECHNI-CALLY, ARTISTICALLY, SOCIALLY AND ECONOMICALLY TO A LEVEL OF SOPHISTICATION FAR BEYOND THE CONCEPTS AND ATTITUDES OF THE ORIGINAL PHOTOGRAPHIC ARTISTS WHO ESTABLISHED PHOTOGRAPHY AS AN ART FORM.

PHOTOGRAPHY HAS GROWN INTO A VERY COMPLEX NETWORK OF ARTISTIC PERSUA-SIONS, WITH SUPPORT AND CONCERN FROM INSTITUTIONS DEDICATED TO PHOTOGRAPHY, WITH A HIGHLY SOPHISTICATED VISUALLY-ORIENTED AUDIENCE.

THE FOLLOWING INTERVIEWS WERE CONDUCTED SPONTANEOUSLY. NO PRE-CONCEIVED RESPONSES WERE ESTABLISHED BY ANY OF THE INDIVIDUALS INTERVIEWED. THE QUESTIONS, HOWEVER, WERE PRE-CONCEIVED.

ALL OF THE PEOPLE INTERVIEWED WERE ASKED THE SAME QUESTIONS, IN THE SAME ORDER, IN HOPES OF ESTABLISHING VARIOUS "PERSPECTIVES" IN RELATION TO THE EVOLUTION, BOTH AESTHETICALLY AND CULTURALLY, OF PHOTOGRAPHY. AN ATTEMPT TO ESTABLISH THE PRESENT STATE OF THE ART OF PHOTOGRAPHY WAS ALSO A MAJOR CONCERN.

THE PHOTOGRAPHERS QUESTIONED WERE UNAWARE OF THE RESPONSES OF THE OTHER PHOTOGRAPHERS, UNTIL AFTER THEY RESPONDED TO THE INTERVIEWER. IT IS REMARKABLE HOW THE JARGON, VERBIAGE AND SOME OF THE OVERALL RESPONSES ARE SO SIMILAR TO ONE ANOTHER, EVEN THOUGH NONE OF THE PHOTOGRAPHERS QUESTIONED HAD PRIOR KNOWLEDGE OF THE OTHER PHOTOGRAPHER'S RESPONSES.

THE FOLLOWING PHOTOGRAPHS ARE ALSO "PERSPECTIVES." ALL PEOPLE PERCEIVE REALITY DIFFERENTLY, AND AS A RESULT, VARIOUS PHOTOGRAPHS OF DIVERGENT SITUATIONS DEPICTING REALITY FROM DIFFERENT STANDPOINTS ARE DISPLAYED FACE TO FACE, IN ORDER TO PRESENT DIFFERENT "PERSPECTIVES" OF THE SAME SITUATION.

WE OVERLOOK MOST OF REALITY.

MANY NUANCES ARE MISSED.

SOMETIMES ENTIRE SEGMENTS OF OUR EXPERIENCES ARE BLOCKED FROM OUR MINDS. OUR MINDS ARE INTRICATE FILTERING SYSTEMS, RECEIVING AND EDITING DIFFERENT SEGMENTS OF OUR EXPERIENCES. THE PERCEPTIONS WHICH ARE FILTERED OUT AND FILTERED IN FROM OUR EXPERIENCE, ARE THE SUBJECT OF "PERSPECTIVES."

ANSEL ADAMS

BORN 1902
BEGAN PHOTOGRAPHY 1916

QUESTION # 1: HOW DO YOU FEEL PHOTOGRAPHY HAS CHANGED, AS AN ART FORM,
DURING YOUR LIFE?

ANSWER: I'VE ALWAYS THOUGHT IT WAS AN ART FORM, BUT IT HAD VERY LOW
APPRECIATION IN THE BEGINNING, EXCEPT FOR SOME EUROPEANS, AND OF COURSE,
STIEGLITZ. STIEGLITZ ALWAYS CONSIDERED PHOTOGRAPHY TO BE AN ART FORM AND
IS THE "FATHER" OF THE CREATIVE CONCEPTS OF THE TWENTIETH CENTURY. I DO
NOT THINK THERE IS ANY QUESTION OF PHOTOGRAPHY BEING AN ART FORM!
     I WOULD SAY THE SECOND PHOTOGRAPHIC RENAISSANCE BEGAN IN THE
EARLY 30's WITH THE F/64 GROUP AND THROUGH THE EXPANSION OF WESTON'S WORK
AND OTHERS. THERE STILL IS SOME OPPOSITION TO IT IN SOME MUSEUMS AND ART
SCHOOLS, BUT I THINK PHOTOGRAPHY HAS REALLY GROWN INTO A MATURE ART FORM.
     THE EVALUATION OF THE HISTORY OF PHOTOGRAPHY, AND JUST WHAT REALLY
DID TAKE PLACE IN THE PAST 150 YEARS IS DIFFICULT FOR ME TO SAY. A FINE
ART HISTORIAN CAN UNRAVEL IT.

QUESTION # 2: DO YOU FEEL THE MOTIVATIONS OF YOUNG PHOTOGRAPHERS DIFFER
FROM YOUR ORIGINAL MOTIVATIONS?

ANSWER: OH, IN DIRECTIONS, BUT NOT IN THE BASIC INTENTIONS OF ART! NOW
THEY ARE DEPARTING FROM THE STRICT, STRAIGHT PHOTOGRAPHY THAT WE PROMOTED
IN THE 30's AND 40's. THEY'RE GOING INTO EXPERIMENTS AND NEW IDEAS; SOME
OF WHICH ARE VERY HANDSOME.
     I THINK WE CANNOT CATEGORIZE. THINGS DO NOT FIT INTO A MOLD.
PHOTOGRAPHY AND PHOTOGRAPHERS HAVE AN INEVITABLE DEVELOPMENT. THEY PRO-
GRESS MORE OR LESS BY STEPS. EVERY FIVE OR TEN YEARS, SOME NEW POINT OF
VIEW IS DEVELOPED AND YOUNG PEOPLE ARE INCLINED TO FOLLOW IT.
     IT WOULD TAKE A CRITIC OR SOMEONE REALLY TRAINED IN HISTORICAL
RESEARCH TO ANALYZE IT. I COULDN'T -- I'M JUST A PHOTOGRAPHER!

QUESTION # 3: HOW DO THE GALLERIES FOR PHOTOGRAPHY TODAY COMPARE WITH THE
PHOTOGRAPHIC GALLERIES WHEN YOU FIRST BEGAN TO EXHIBIT?

ANSWER: WHEN I BEGAN THERE WEREN'T ANY GALLERIES FOR PHOTOGRAPHY THAT I
KNEW OF, OTHER THAN STIEGLITZ'S CENTER, WHICH WASN'T A TRUE GALLERY. IT
WAS MORE OF A "LABORATORY." I DO NOT KNOW WHAT WAS IN EUROPE, BUT AS I
MAKE OUT, THERE WERE VERY FEW REAL GALLERIES DEVOTED TO PHOTOGRAPHY. THIS
WAS DURING THE 30's.
     NOW, THERE IS A BIG TURNOVER IN THE GALLERIES. THE TOP GALLERIES
ARE GETTING BETTER ALL THE TIME. A LOT OF GALLERIES JUST STRUGGLE ALONG,
AND THERE ARE GALLERIES WHICH COME AND GO. THEY OPEN AND CLOSE, THEN A
NEW ONE COMES ALONG. THERE IS CERTAINLY A GREAT NUMBER OF GALLERIES. I
THINK THIS ARGUES WELL FOR THE ART, BUT, THERE ARE, OF COURSE, A LOT OF
"PHONIES," AS WITH ALL THE ARTS.

QUESTION # 4: WHY DID YOU CALL STIEGLITZ'S GALLERY A "LABORATORY" OR
EXPERIMENT?

ANSWER: HE WAS AVIDLY DEVOTED TO THE IDEA OF PHOTOGRAPHY AS AN ART FORM.
THERE WAS THE FIFTH AVENUE GALLERY AND THEN THERE WAS THE AMERICAN PLACE

ON MADISON AVENUE. THEY WERE NOT COMMERCIAL GALLERIES. HE SHOWED,
IN THE BEGINNING, SOME FOR THE FIRST TIME, MANY OF THE GREATEST CONTEMPOR-
ARY ARTISTS, AND HE DEVELOPED HIS OWN GROUP: O'KEEFE, DOVE AND OTHERS.
HIS WAS NOT A COMMERCIAL GALLERY. HE WAS A NON-COMMERCIAL KNIGHT IN ARMOR,
WHO CONCEIVED OF PHOTOGRAPHY AS ART, ALONG WITH THE OTHER MEDIUMS.

QUESTION # 5:   DO YOU THINK PHOTOGRAPHY HAS BECOME "BIG BUSINESS?"

ANSWER: WELL, I THINK PHOTOGRAPHY IS BEING RECOGNIZED AND COLLECTED.
ITS VALUES HAVE CERTAINLY GONE UP AND CONTINUE TO GO UP.
        THE OLD PHOTOGRAPHS, SUCH AS CAMERON AND OTHER LATER 19th CENTURY
PHOTOGRAPHERS, AFTER THE DAGUERREOTYPE, ARE VERY VALUABLE, CHIEFLY BECAUSE
THEY ARE VERY SCARCE.
        THERE ARE PEOPLE WHO ARE MORE MODERN, LIKE STRAND, CAPONIGRO,
AND WESTON, WHO ARE VERY IMPORTANT IN THE SALES ASPECTS. I DO VERY WELL
AND THERE ARE SOME YOUNG PEOPLE COMING UP. IT IS VERY ENCOURAGING IN
THAT RESPECT. THE PHOTOGRAPHERS AND THE ARTISTS CONTRIBUTE A LOT TO THE
WORLD AND HAVE A RIGHT TO EXIST IN RELATIVE SECURITY AND COMFORT.

QUESTION # 6:   DO YOU FEEL FINE ART PHOTOGRAPHY, WHEN YOU BEGAN WAS AN
                "UNDERGROUND" ACTIVITY,WITH ONLY A FEW PEOPLE INVOLVED?

ANSWER: YES, RELATIVELY FEW AT THE CREATIVE LEVEL; HOWEVER, THE TERM
"UNDERGROUND" REALLY DOES NOT APPLY.

QUESTION # 7:   HOW DO YOU PERCEIVE THE INFLUX IN PHOTOGRAPHY?

ANSWER: PHOTOGRAPHY HAS ESCALATED ALMOST EXPONENTIALLY! IT IS A LANGUAGE
WHICH COVERS ALMOST EVERY ASPECT OF COMMUNICATION -- FACTUAL AND EXPRESSIVE.
        THE PHOTO-JOURNALIST, THE PHOTO-POET ARE BOTH IMPORTANT. THE
PROBLEM IS TO SEPARATE THE MAJOR OBJECTIVES OF THE VARIOUS GROUPS, AND
NOT ATTRIBUTE QUALITIES AND INTENTIONS WHERE THEY DO NOT BELONG.
        I THINK DOROTHEA LANGE BRIDGED THE SPACE BETWEEN PHOTO-DOCUMEN-
TATION AND PHOTO-POETRY TO AN EXTRAORDINARY DEGREE. THERE ARE FEW SUCH
EXAMPLES!

JERRY UELSMAN

BORN 1934
STARTED PHOTOGRAPHY 1947-8

QUESTION # 1:   HOW DO YOU FEEL PHOTOGRAPHY, AS AN ART FORM, HAS CHANGED
IN YOUR LIFE TIME?

ANSWER: I THINK PEOPLE'S PERCEPTION OF PHOTOGRAPHY, AS AN ART FORM, HAS
CHANGED RADICALLY IN MY LIFE TIME; AND AS A RESULT, A LARGER AUDIENCE FOR
PHOTOGRAPHY HAS EVOLVED! A GREATER NUMBER OF PEOPLE ARE USING THE MEDIUM
SERIOUSLY.
I THINK PHOTOGRAPHY BECAME MORE INVOLVED IN THE UNIVERSITY SYSTEM,
SO THAT PHOTOGRAPHERS HAD MORE CONTACT WITH OTHER ARTISTS, AND THERE WAS
A HEALTHY INTERCHANGE, WHICH MADE MANY PEOPLE AWARE OF HOW VIABLE THE
MEDIUM REALLY IS.   CURRENTLY, I FEEL, THERE IS A RENAISSANCE IN PHOTOGRAPHY!
AN EXAMPLE OF PHOTOGRAPHY'S EVOLUTION CAN BE SEEN IN THE S.P.S.
(THE SOCIETY FOR PHOTOGRAPHIC EDUCATION). I WAS ONE OF THE FOUNDING MEMBERS,
AND AT THAT TIME, WE COULD HAVE ALL MET IN A PHONE BOOTH. NOW, THERE ARE
SEVEN, EIGHT HUNDRED OR A THOUSAND MEMBERS.

QUESTION # 2:   HOW DO YOU FEEL PHOTOGRAPHY HAS CHANGED, FROM THE STANDPOINT
OF AESTHETICS?

ANSWER: AESTHETICALLY, I THINK THE BIGGEST CHANGE HAS BEEN THAT WE ARE
NO LONGER CONCERNED WITH HOW A PHOTOGRAPH MUST LOOK!
I THINK IN THE EARLY FIFTIES CONCERN FOR THE "ZONE SYSTEM" WAS
EMERGING. A MYTHICAL-ARCHETYPAL PRINT QUALITY WAS BEING PROMOTED.   IT
WAS THE MODEL OF HOW A PHOTOGRAPH SHOULD LOOK.
I THINK IN THE LAST TWENTY YEARS THINGS HAVE OPENED UP CONSIDER-
ABLY. YOU CAN NOW HAVE PEOPLE LIKE ROBERT HEINECKEN, ANSEL ADAMS AND MY-
SELF, ALL USING LIGHT SENSITIVE MATERIALS DIFFERENTLY, AND STILL, ALL PART
OF THE WORLD OF PHOTOGRAPHY.
AESTHETICALLY, PHOTOGRAPHY IS A LOT LESS UPTIGHT ABOUT PROVING
ITSELF AS AN ART FORM. NOW THE MEDIUM HAS BECOME A LOT MORE ACCESSIBLE TO
CREATIVE PEOPLE IN GENERAL, AND AS A RESULT, THERE IS A WEALTH OF EXCITING
EXPERIMENTATION.

QUESTION # 3:   DO YOU FEEL THE MOTIVATIONS OF YOUNG PHOTOGRAPHERS TODAY
DIFFER FROM YOUR ORIGINAL MOTIVATIONS AND CONCERNS WITH
PHOTOGRAPHY?

ANSWER: YOU CAN NOT CATEGORICALLY SAY ANYTHING ABOUT YOUNG PHOTOGRAPHERS.
I FIND SOME YOUNG PHOTOGRAPHERS HAVE CONCERNS NOT UNLIKE MY OWN.   I DO
THINK, HOWEVER, THERE ARE SOME YOUNG PEOPLE WHO HAVE HAD DIFFERENT ART
INFLUENCES AND THEY ARE ABLE TO RELATE MORE INTENSELY THAN I CAN TO SOME
OF THE CONCEPT ART AND SOME OF THE MORE CONTEMPORARY MOVEMENTS IN ART.

QUESTION # 4:   DO YOU THINK PHOTOGRAPHY HAS BECOME "BIG BUSINESS?"

ANSWER: "BIG BUSINESS" AS COMPARED TO WHAT?
IT CERTAINLY HAS BECOME BIG BUSINESS, COMPARED TO WHAT IT WAS.
AN EXAMPLE WOULD BE -- TEN YEARS AGO IF YOU OFFERED ME AN EXHIBIT IN A
MEN'S ROOM, I WOULD HAVE HUNG IT MYSELF! TODAY I GET LETTERS EVERYDAY
REQUESTING SHOWS. I CAN NOT POSSIBLY ANSWER ALL MY MAIL; LET ALONE DEAL
WITH SHOW REQUESTS.

I DO THINK ONCE YOU HAVE ESTABLISHED PHOTOGRAPHY AS A VIABLE
VEHICLE, IT IS ONLY NATURAL THAT ENTREPRENEURS ARE GOING TO GET INVOLVED
WITH THE MEDIUM. SOME OF THEM ARE VERY SENSITIVE PEOPLE, AND SOME OF THEM,
LIKE ANY BUSINESS, ARE OUT TO GET THE BUCK. THE FACT THAT ENTREPRENEURS
ARE SPECULATING IN PHOTOGRAPHY AND CERTAIN PHOTOGRAPHERS HAVE BUSINESS
MANAGERS, IS EVIDENCE THAT PHOTOGRAPHY, IN SOME CASES, IS BECOMING BIG
BUSINESS!

QUESTION # 5:   HOW DO THE GALLERIES FOR PHOTOGRAPHY TODAY COMPARE WITH
                THE PHOTOGRAPHIC GALLERIES WHEN YOU FIRST BEGAN TO EXHIBIT?

ANSWER: WELL, THERE WERE NOT ANY BACK THEN, WITH THE POSSIBLE EXCEPTION
OF THE LIMELIGHT IN NEW YORK.
         THE FIRST SHOW THAT I WAS PART OF, IN THE CONTEXT OF SERIOUS
PHOTOGRAPHY, WAS AT THE EASTMAN HOUSE. THEY HAD PUT TOGETHER A SHOW
ENTITLED, "PHOTOGRAPHY AT MID-CENTURY." THAT SHOW MUST HAVE BEEN ABOUT
1958.
         THE SIMBAB GALLERY, IN BOSTON, AND THE WITKIN GALLERY IN NEW
YORK STARTED ABOUT TEN YEARS AGO. THERE ARE NOW AT LEAST SOME MORE QUALITY
GALLERIES, LIKE THE SIMBAB AND THE WITKIN, DEVELOPING INTO PROFESSIONAL
GALLERIES.
         THERE ARE A LOT OF YOUNG PEOPLE WHO NAIVELY ASSUME THEY CAN OPEN
A GALLERY AND PEOPLE ARE GOING TO BEAT THEIR WAY TO THEIR DOOR TO BUY
ART. THEY DO NOT REALIZE THE COST OF RUNNING A GALLERY -- THE SPACE,
LIGHTING, INSURANCE, SHIPPING, THE CARE AND MAINTENANCE OF THE WORK. IT
CAN BE VERY DEMANDING.
         NOW, WE HAVE GALLERIES WHICH HAVE EXCELLENT REPUTATIONS, AND I
ALSO THINK, THAT A LOT OF ESTABLISHED PAINTING GALLERIES ARE NOW BEGINNING
TO EXHIBIT PHOTOGRAPHS IN ORDER TO GET ON THE BAND WAGON.

QUESTION # 6:   IF YOU HAVE EVER ATTEMPTED TO EXHIBIT IN A GALLERY WHICH
                WAS NOT DEDICATED TO PHOTOGRAPHY (AN "ART GALLERY), WHAT
                WAS THE RESPONSE?

ANSWER: I HAVE NEVER GONE OUT OF MY WAY TO GET GALLERIES. THEY HAVE
ALWAYS CONTACTED ME; BUT, I RECENTLY SHOWED IN GALLERIES WHICH DO NOT
TRADITIONALLY SHOW PHOTOGRAPHY, OR HAVE ONLY OCCASIONALLY SHOWN PHOTO-
GRAPHY, AND THE RESPONSE HAS BEEN GOOD.
         I THINK ONE OF THE PROBLEMS THAT DEVELOPED OVER THE YEARS WAS
A KIND OF INGRAINED IDEA -- PHOTOGRAPHY FOR PHOTOGRAPHERS.
MUCH OF WHAT HAPPENS TODAY IN PHOTOGRAPHY IS VIEWED AND APPRECIATED BY
A GREATER AUDIENCE THAN WE REALIZE.

QUESTION # 7:   DO YOU PERCEIVE AN INFLUX IN PHOTOGRAPHY AND IF YOU DO,
                COULD YOU PLEASE CHARACTERIZE IT?

ANSWER: I WOULD SAY WE ARE IN A VERY STRONG GROWTH PERIOD RIGHT NOW.
THERE IS A TREMENDOUS INTEREST IN PHOTOGRAPHY AS A MEDIUM. PHOTOGRAPHY
SEEMS TO BE MORE ACCEPTABLE TO THE NEEDS OF THE YOUNG ARTIST TODAY THAN
TRADITIONAL MEDIA. IT REQUIRES LESS DISCIPLINE BEFORE YOU GET AN ACTUAL
IMAGE. THERE IS A LOT OF IMMEDIACY WITH THE LIGHT SENSITIVE MATERIALS.
THE RESULTS OCCUR IN A QUICKER FORM THAN THEY DO IF YOU ARE PAINTING OR
SCULPTING. I THINK THIS HAS A LOT OF APPEAL TO ENERGETIC AND INTELLIGENT
YOUNG PEOPLE.

HOWEVER, I AM NOT TRYING TO SAY THERE IS ANY HIERARCHY IN THE ARTS, AS TO ONE MEDIA BEING BETTER; BUT, I DO THINK PHOTOGRAPHY HAS INTEGRATED ITSELF VERY WELL INTO THE ART SCENE!

I THINK, IN GENERAL TERMS, THERE IS A TREMENDOUS GROWTH RIGHT NOW IN PHOTOGRAPHY. IN MOST OF THE UNIVERSITIES I VISIT, THERE ARE LONG WAITING LISTS FOR PEOPLE INTERESTED IN BEGINNING PHOTOGRAPHY COURSES.

I ALSO THINK, FROM THE HUMANISTIC POINT OF VIEW, THAT PEOPLE BENEFIT GREATLY FROM THEIR INVOLVEMENT WITH THE MEDIUM; BUT, I DO NOT THINK THEY ARE ALL GOING TO GO OUT AND SURVIVE AS ARTISTS!

QUESTION # 8:   DO YOU FEEL FINE ART PHOTOGRAPHY, WHEN YOU BEGAN, WAS AN "UNDERGROUND" ACTIVITY, WITH ONLY A FEW PEOPLE INVOLVED?

ANSWER: YES, I GUESS I DO. THE WORD "UNDERGROUND" HAS CERTAIN CONNOTA- TIONS WHICH DO NOT APPLY; BUT, IT WAS DEFINITELY A KIND OF "UNDERGROUND."

THE PEOPLE INVOLVED WERE VERY MUCH LIKE A BIG FAMILY. A LOT OF PEOPLE KNEW EACH OTHER. THERE WERE SO FEW PEOPLE INVOLVED WITH FINE ART PHOTOGRAPHY, THAT IT WAS POSSIBLE TO BE AWARE OF WHAT WAS GOING ON.

QUESTION # 9:   IS THERE AN "ESTABLISHED" POINT OF VIEW VERSUS AN "AVANT- GARDE" POINT OF VIEW IN FINE ART PHOTOGRAPHY, AND IF YOU THINK THERE IS, PLEASE CHARACTERIZE IT?

ANSWER: I THINK PRACTICING PHOTOGRAPHERS, WHO ARE NOT TEACHING, ARE MORE INCLINED TO HAVE A DEFINITIVE AESTHETIC STANCE.

WHEN I TEACH, I SPEND A GREAT DEAL OF TIME TRYING TO SHARE THE JOYS OF DIFFERENT PHOTOGRAPHERS, SO I END UP TALKING A LOT ABOUT ANSEL ADAMS, STIELGLITZ, DUANE MICHAELS AND MANY OTHERS. AS A RESULT, I GAIN APPRECIATION FOR MANY DIFFERENT AESTHETIC VIEW POINTS. I DO NOT TRY TO PROMOTE ANY PARTICULAR AESTHETIC STANCE -- TRADITIONAL OR NON-TRADITIONAL.

I TRY TO KEEP ABREAST OF WHAT IS HAPPENING TODAY IN PHOTOGRAPHY AS BEST I CAN; BUT, AS YOU KNOW, THE AVANT-GARDE OF TODAY IS THE REAR- GARDE OF TOMORROW. I TRY TO KEEP IN TOUCH WITH THE KINDS OF CONCERNS ART IS ADDRESSING ITSELF TO IN MY TIME!

RALPH GIBSON

BORN JANUARY 16, 1939
STARTED PHOTOGRAPHY IN U.S. NAVY - 1956

QUESTION # 1:   HOW DO YOU FEEL PHOTOGRAPHY, AS AN ART FORM, HAS CHANGED
                IN YOUR LIFE TIME?

ANSWER: WELL, IT HAD CONSIDERABLE IMPACT ON THE NATURE OF HOW I PERCEIVE
REALITY AND MYSELF, BECAUSE THROUGH THE YEARS THERE HAVE BEEN CERTAIN
CONSTANTS IN MY WORK -- THINGS THAT I HAVE COME TO SEE AND TRUST.
        I HAVE ARRIVED AT THE PLACE WHERE THE THINGS I TRUST MOST IN MY
LIFE ARE WHAT I SEE REFLECTED IN MY WORK. THE REST OF THE TIME, I'M A
HIGHLY ERRATIC FELLOW, BUT THE PHOTOGRAPHS PROBABLY SAY PRETTY MUCH WHAT
I MEAN.

QUESTION # 2:   HOW DO YOU FEEL, IN GENERAL TERMS, THE AESTHETICS OF PHOTO-
                GRAPHY HAVE CHANGED IN YOUR EXPERIENCE OF PHOTOGRAPHY?

ANSWER: WELL, IN THE TWENTY YEARS THAT I HAVE BEEN WORKING, I WATCHED
PHOTOGRAPHY GO THROUGH ANY NUMBER OF DEFINITIONS. IT'S AT THE POINT NOW
WHERE AESTHETICS ARE CENTERED AROUND THE IDEA OF EXPANDING THE DEFINITION
OF THE MEDIUM, AS OPPOSED TO IT BEING CONSIDERED A FIRM TRADITION.
        THE MEDIUM NOW HAS THE RECOGNITION OF AN ART FORM. IT IS BECOMING
POSSIBLE TO DO ANY NUMBER OF DIFFERENT KINDS OF THINGS, WHICH HAVEN'T
BEEN ACTUALLY CONSIDERED AND REGARDED. I THINK WE OWE A LOT OF THIS AWARE-
NESS TO THE FACT THAT THINGS LIKE LIFE MAGAZINE AND TELEVISION PREPARED
OUR CULTURE SO THAT WE ARE HIGHLY SOPHISTICATED-- VISUALLY. NOW PEOPLE
ARE PREPARED TO CONSIDER A LOT MORE. AT ONE TIME IT WAS LANDSCAPE, THEN
IT MOVED INTO THE DOCUMENTARY IMAGE, AND THEN IT MOVED INTO PHOTO-JOURNAL-
ISM, AND THEN IT MOVED INTO WHATEVER YOU CHOSE TO DO.

QUESTION # 3:   DO YOU FEEL THE MOTIVATIONS OF YOUNG PHOTOGRAPHERS TODAY
                DIFFER FROM YOUR ORIGINAL MOTIVATIONS AND CONCERNS WITH
                PHOTOGRAPHY?

ANSWER: YES, I DO. THE PROBLEM IS SOMEWHAT OF A DOUBLE-EDGED SWORD,
BECAUSE NOW THE CAMERAS, MATERIALS AND THE AUDIENCE ARE ALL VERY AWARE
AND RESPONSIVE. AS A RESULT, I SEE MANY YOUNG PHOTOGRAPHERS IN THEIR
EARLY TWENTIES DEMAND A GREAT DEAL OF ATTENTION, AND CONSIDER THEIR OWN
WORK IN VERY HIGH REGARD. SOME OF THEM ARE NOT WILLING TO TAKE THE TIME
PERHAPS OTHERS HAVE FOUND IT NECESSARY TO TAKE, TO DEVELOP THEIR WORK. I
MEAN, NOW WE HAVE SUCH A SOPHISTICATED MEDIA CULTURE, PEOPLE WANT TO PASS
THROUGH VERY QUICKLY, AND I THINK MOST YOUNG PHOTOGRAPHERS HAVE THE TEND-
ENCY TO GO OFF HALF-COCKED. MINOR WHITE SAID, QUITE VIVIDLY, THAT IT
TAKES FIFTEEN YEARS TO BECOME A GOOD PHOTOGRAPHER; BUT, IT TAKES FIFTEEN
YEARS TO BECOME A GOOD PLUMBER, OR A GOOD DENTIST, OR LAWYER OR CARPENTER.

QUESTION # 4:   DO YOU THINK FINE ART PHOTOGRAPHY HAS BECOME "BIG BUSINESS?"

ANSWER: I DON'T THINK PHOTOGRAPHY HAS OR WILL EVER BECOME "BIG BUSINESS,"
IF YOU COMPARE IT WITH THE ART WORLD IN GENERAL. PEOPLE MIGHT FEEL SOME
KIND OF ANTIPATHY, I DON'T KNOW WHY, THAT A PHOTOGRAPHER CAN MAKE A LIVING
NOW FROM THE SALE OF HIS PRINTS, SUCH AS I DO. HOWEVER, IT'S NEVER GOING
TO BE THE SAME KIND OF LIVING AS A MAJOR PAINTER, OR MAJOR SCULPTOR, OR
MAJOR MUSICIAN, OR MAJOR DANCER IS GOING TO MAKE, BECAUSE REGARDLESS OF

HOW VALUABLE THESE PHOTOGRAPHS ARE GOING TO BECOME, FOR THE MOST PART,
THEY ARE NOT AS VALUABLE AS A THIRD-RATE PAINTING.

QUESTION # 5:   HOW DO THE GALLERIES FOR PHOTOGRAPHY TODAY COMPARE WITH
                THE PHOTOGRAPHIC GALLERIES WHEN YOU FIRST BEGAN TO EXHIBIT?

ANSWER: FOR ONE THING, THE GALLERIES OF TODAY ARE SHOWING PHOTOGRAPHS BE-
CAUSE IT IS A CREATIVE THING FOR THE GALLERIES TO DO. THE GALLERY DEALER
GETS TO EXERCISE SOME OF HIS OR HER CREATIVITY.
        COLLECTORS ARE NOW GETTING INTO PHOTOGRAPHY BECAUSE THEY CAN
USE THEIR OWN TASTE, THEIR OWN HUNCH, THEIR OWN INTUITION IN WHAT THEY
LIKE, AND THE PRICES ARE ACCOMMODATING. THESE COLLECTORS PREVIOUSLY HAD
TO SPEND THOUSANDS AND THOUSANDS OF DOLLARS FOR A PAINTING. NOW THEY CAN
BUILD A MAJOR PHOTOGRAPHY COLLECTION FOR CONSIDERABLY LESS MONEY, AND HAVE
MORE FUN DOING IT.
        THERE IS SUCH A THING AS A CREATIVE DEALER AND A CREATIVE COLLECTOR.
I SEE COLLECTIONS THAT ARE WORTH A LOT OF MONEY, PAINTINGS AND SCULPTURES
THAT AREN'T VERY GOOD COLLECTIONS, AND I SEE OTHER COLLECTIONS THAT ARE
EXQUISITE. THE SAME THING IS TRUE OF GALLERIES -- SOME DEALERS WILL JUST
SELL YOU ANYTHING THEY CAN MOVE, AND OTHER DEALERS WILL BALANCE INTO YOUR
COLLECTION.
        THERE IS CERTAINLY LESS RISK INVOLVED FOR DEALERS NOW THAN BEFORE,
IN TERMS OF WHAT IT COSTS THEM TO PUT ON A SHOW. BEFORE, SHOWS WERE
CRITICAL SUCCESSES, BUT THE DEALER GENERALLY LOST MONEY. THIS IS MORE
LIKE SIX OR SEVEN YEARS AGO. NOW, THE MORE DYNAMIC DEALERS HAVE BEEN ABLE
TO STIMULATE THEIR COLLECTORS AND THINGS HAVE BEEN GETTING MORE INTERESTING
THAT WAY. CONSEQUENTLY, ONE HAS THE OPPORTUNITY TO SHOW MORE.
        I HAVE ABOUT FIFTEEN ONE MAN SHOWS A YEAR AROUND THE WORLD, AND
IT IS VERY RARE THAT NOTHING IS ACQUIRED BY COLLECTORS. IN FACT, THERE IS
ALWAYS SOMETHING ACQUIRED! PERHAPS FIVE OR SEVEN YEARS AGO IT WOULD BE
LESS EXTRAORDINARY TO HAVE NOTHING SOLD.

QUESTION # 6:   IF YOU HAVE EVER ATTEMPTED TO EXHIBIT IN A GALLERY, WHICH
                WAS NOT DEDICATED TO PHOTOGRAPHY (AN "ART GALLERY"), WHAT
                WAS THE RESPONSE?

ANSWER: I'M MORE INTERESTED IN SHOWING IN FINE ART GALLERIES THAN SPECIF-
ICALLY PHOTOGRAPHY GALLERIES BECAUSE THE NATURE OF MY CONCERNS WITHIN MY
PHOTOGRAPHIC WORK IS SUCH THAT, GENERALLY SPEAKING, THE AUDIENCE IN AN
ART GALLERY IS BETTER PREPARED TO UNDERSTAND WHAT I'M DOING.

QUESTION # 7:   WHY WOULD THAT BE?

ANSWER: BECAUSE THE HISTORY OF ART IS THREE THOUSAND YEARS OLD. PHOTO-
GRAPHY ESSENTIALLY DEALS WITH THE THREE DIMENSIONAL REALITY, PORTRAYED ON
A TWO DIMENSIONAL PICTURE PLANE. THE AESTHETICS OF PHOTOGRAPHY ARE IN
THEIR INFANCY. ON THE OTHER HAND, THERE ARE THREE THOUSAND YEARS OF ART
HISTORY AND INFORMATION CENTERED AROUND DEALING WITH THE TWO DIMENSIONAL
PICTURE PLANE AS A CONCERN.

QUESTION # 8:   DO YOU PERCEIVE AN INFLUX IN PHOTOGRAPHY, AND IF YOU DO,
                PLEASE CHARACTERIZE IT?

ANSWER: OH, OF COURSE, THE MEDIUM IS COMPLETELY CHANGING. FOR EXAMPLE: IF I WERE TO ASK YOU WHAT WAS THE STATE OF THE ART IN PHOTOGRAPHY FIFTY YEARS AGO, IT WOULD BE EASY TO ANSWER, IF I COULD SAY WHAT THE MOST RELEVANT CONCERNS WERE IN THE MEDIA IN 1900. NOW, WITH A HISTORICAL PERSPECTIVE, WE CAN ANSWER THAT QUESTION QUITE CLEARLY.

WHAT I'M INTERESTED IN RIGHT NOW, IN THE MIDDLE OF ALL THIS TREMENDOUS ACTIVITY, IS -- I WOULD LIKE TO ASCERTAIN, WHAT IS THE STATE OF THE ART OF PHOTOGRAPHY TODAY? WHAT EXACTLY ARE THE MOST RELEVANT ISSUES THAT ARE BEING ADDRESSED?

I THINK THAT IT IS A VERY COMPLEX AND INTERESTING PROBLEM, WHICH I GIVE A GREAT DEAL OF THOUGHT TO, AND I FEEL THAT, IN FACT, SOME ISSUES IN PHOTOGRAPHY ARE MORE VALID TO PURSUE, IN TERMS OF THIS QUESTION, THAN OTHERS. I DON'T PARTICULARLY FEEL, IN TERMS OF MY OWN NEEDS, THAT IT IS LEGITIMATE FOR ME TO GO OVER GROUND THAT HAS ALREADY BEEN COVERED.

QUESTION # 9:   LET'S TAKE IT FROM THE STANDPOINT OF ECONOMY. HAS THERE BEEN AN INFLUX IN PHOTOGRAPHY, ECONOMICALLY?

ANSWER: OF COURSE. WELL, AS YOU KNOW THERE HAS BEEN A TREMENDOUS AMOUNT OF RESEARCH AND TECHNOLOGICAL DEVELOPMENT THAT HAS CENTERED AROUND THE REFINEMENT OF THE MATERIALS IN THE MEDIUM. WE KNOW THE FINE ART ASPECT OF PHOTOGRAPHY IS VERY SMALL, COMPARED WITH THE INDUSTRY. ALL THIS TECHNOLOGICAL ADVANCEMENT, AT THE SAME TIME, HAS TURNED OUT TO BE MUCH TO THE ADVANTAGE OF THE CONTEMPORARY WORKER.

QUESTION # 10:   DO YOU FEEL FINE ART PHOTOGRAPHY, WHEN YOU BEGAN, WAS AN "UNDERGROUND" ACTIVITY, WITH ONLY A FEW PEOPLE INVOLVED?

ANSWER: YES, I DO, VERY MUCH SO. I FEEL AND REMEMBER, AS RECENTLY AS 1969, EIGHT YEARS AGO, THE MAJOR THRUST OF MY EXCHANGE HAD TO DO WITH A VERY SMALL PEER GROUP IN NEW YORK THAT MET REGULARLY. NOW, THERE IS A MUCH WIDER RANGE OF SOCIAL INTERCOURSE, SHALL WE SAY..

QUESTION # 11:   HOW WERE YOU CIRCULATING YOUR WORK AT THAT TIME?

ANSWER: I WASN'T. I WORKED IN THE CLOSET FOR THE FIRST TWELVE YEARS OF MY CAREER. THIS FORCED ME TO WORK COMMERCIALLY, WHICH I HATED.

QUESTION # 12:   HAS THE CIRCULATION OF YOUR FINE ART PHOTOGRAPHY MADE IT POSSIBLE FOR YOU TO STOP DOING COMMERCIAL PHOTOGRAPHY?

ANSWER: YES. I HAVEN'T DONE ANY COMMERCIAL WORK SINCE 1970, SINCE THE PUBLICATION OF THE SOMNAMBULIST.

QUESTION # 13:   IS THERE AN "ESTABLISHED" POINT OF VIEW, OPPOSED TO AN "AVANT-GARDE" POINT OF VIEW IN FINE ART PHOTOGRAPHY, AND IF YOU THINK THERE IS, PLEASE CHARACTERIZE IT?

ANSWER: WELL, I THINK THERE IS AN "ESTABLISHED" POINT OF VIEW-- HOWEVER, I DON'T THINK WE HAVE AN ACADEMY.

I THINK THERE IS A TREMENDOUS AMOUNT OF DISCUSSION GOING ON BETWEEN THE SO-CALLED "PURIST" APPROACH OR THE DOCUMENTARY IMAGE, WHICH IS A VERY OBJECTIVE APPROACH, AND THE MORE SUBJECTIVE WORKERS. I THINK THERE IS SOMEWHAT OF A DICHOTOMY THERE, AND I THINK THAT IT'S VERY, VERY GOOD THAT IT EXISTS.

I FIND THAT IF EVERYONE THOUGHT THE SAME ABOUT PHOTOGRAPHY, IT WOULD BE VERY DULL AND WE COULDN'T HAVE THE ENORMOUS AMOUNT OF ACTIVITY THAT WE DO HAVE NOW. WE DO HAVE SEVERAL DIFFERENT SCHOOLS. AND THERE ARE A LOT OF PEOPLE WHO BELIEVE THAT ONE WAY IS RIGHT, AND OTHER PEOPLE WHO BELIEVE ANOTHER WAY IS RIGHT. MY PERSONAL FEELINGS ARE THAT I HAVE A LOT OF RESPECT FOR ANY KIND OF A PHOTOGRAPH THAT IS DIFFICULT TO DO AND IS DONE WELL. I FEEL THAT MAKING A GOOD PHOTOGRAPH IN ANY GENRE IS A CONSIDERABLE UNDER-TAKING, AND I CAN'T HELP BUT RESPECT THE RESULTS.

QUESTION # 14: DO YOU HAVE ANYTHING YOU WOULD LIKE TO ADD IN RELATION TO WHAT WE HAVE DISCUSSED, OR ANY OTHER MATERIAL YOU WOULD LIKE TO COMMUNICATE? I HAVE NO MORE QUESTIONS!

ANSWER: WELL, RIGHT NOW, IN MY OWN WORK, I'M DEALING WITH PROBLEMS OF ATTEMPTING TO RELY LESS ON THE SUBJECT MATTER. I'M TRYING VERY HARD TO BRING THE PICTURE PLANE FORWARD, AS OPPOSED TO CREATING THE THREE DIMEN-SIONAL PICTURE WINDOW. I'D LIKE THE VISUAL ACTIVITY TO EXIST BETWEEN THE SURFACE OF THE PRINT AND THE VIEWER, WITHOUT THE ILLUSION OF THE ACTIVITY TRANSPIRING FROM THE PICTURE PLANE BACK. I THINK, FOR ME, IN TERMS OF MY OWN EFFORTS, THIS IS A LEGITIMATE CONCERN.

ROBERT HEINECKEN

BORN OCTOBER 29, 1931
STARTED PHOTOGRAPHY TENTATIVELY - 1960
SERIOUSLY   - 1962

QUESTION # 1:   HOW DO YOU FEEL PHOTOGRAPHY, IN YOUR LIFE TIME, HAS CHANGED?

ANSWER: PRIOR TO THE TIME I REALLY BEGAN MAKING PHOTOGRAPHS AND INCORPOR-
ATING THEM INTO ETCHINGS AND OTHER PRINTING MEDIUMS, I WASN'T REALLY
CONSCIOUS OF PHOTOGRAPHY. I PROBABLY WAS NO MORE CONSCIOUS THAN THE
AVERAGE PERSON. SO, PRIOR TO THAT TIME I WASN'T AWARE OF THE SIGNIFICANT
CHANGES THAT HAD GONE ON.
        I SIMPLY WASN'T INTERESTED. I THINK EVERYONE WAS AWARE OF LIFE
MAGAZINE, AND THAT KIND OF PHOTOGRAPHY; BUT, BEFORE I BEGAN MAKING PHOTO-
GRAPHS, I WASN'T CONSCIOUS OF PHOTOGRAPHY AS AN ART FORM AT ALL.

QUESTION # 2:   HOW WOULD SAY PHOTOGRAPHY CHANGED AFTER YOU BECAME INVOLVED
                WITH IT?

ANSWER: WELL, IN THAT PERIOD OF TIME THERE WAS REALLY AN INTERESTING
MULTIPLICATION OF IDEAS IN PHOTOGRAPHY, THAT WASN'T PRESENT INITIALLY IN
THE EARLY SIXTIES, SUCH AS -- LANGUAGE ART IDEAS, WHICH ARE FAIRLY RECENT,
OR THE WHOLE APPROACH TO IT FROM A SOCIOLOGICAL, SUB-CULTURE IDEA. THERE'S
A LOT OF INTERESTING WORK AROUND ABOUT VARIOUS SUB-CULTURES. PHOTO-
GRAPHY IS ALSO SEEN MORE AND MORE AS CONCEPTUAL FORM NOW, AS OPPOSED TO
PHYSICAL FORM. THE EXPANSION, IN THE VERY SHORT PERIOD OF TIME THAT I
HAVE BEEN INVOLVED, IS RATHER REMARKABLE.

QUESTION # 3:   DO YOU FEEL THE MOTIVATIONS OF YOUNG PHOTOGRAPHERS TODAY
                DIFFER FROM YOUR ORIGINAL MOTIVATIONS AND CONCERNS WITH
                PHOTOGRAPHY?

ANSWER: THAT IS AN INTERESTING QUESTION. I THINK, IN SOME WAYS, THEY
MOST LIKELY DON'T DIFFER THAT MUCH. MY EARLY CONCERNS WERE PURELY
EXPLORATORY, WITHOUT THE INITIAL NOTION THAT I WOULD DO ANYTHING WITH IT.
IT WAS REALLY A MATTER OF TRYING OUT PHOTOGRAPHY IN CONNECTION WITH
PRINTMAKING, ON THE SAME BASIS THAT I WAS TRYING OTHER MEDIA AND IDEAS.
IT WAS PURELY A MATTER OF TRYING THINGS TO SEE WHAT WOULD HAPPEN.
        I THINK IT MAY DIFFER A LITTLE BIT NOW. PEOPLE, I THINK, HAVE
THE FEELING THAT THERE IS AT LEAST A COMMUNITY FOR THEM; NOT NECESSARILY
A MARKET. THERE IS A WAY FOR THEM, IF THEY ARE AT ALL AMBITIOUS, TO MAKE
THEIR WORK VISIBLE, AND TO SENSE THERE IS GOING TO BE SOME SUPPORT FOR
THEM; WHEREAS, I NEVER HAD THAT FEELING UNTIL MORE RECENTLY.

QUESTION # 4:   DO YOU FEEL FINE ART PHOTOGRAPHY, WHEN YOU BEGAN, WAS AN
                "UNDERGROUND" ACTIVITY, WITH ONLY A FEW PEOPLE INVOLVED?

ANSWER: YES, I DO. AS I SAID, IT CHANGED VERY RAPIDLY INTO SOMETHING
QUITE DIFFERENT, BUT CERTAINLY NOT UNTIL ABOUT 1967-1968.
        I DON'T THINK THERE WERE A LOT OF PEOPLE INVOLVED. FOR INSTANCE,
I HAD THE IMPRESSION, AT THAT POINT, THAT I KNEW ALMOST EVERYONE WHO WAS
EXHIBITING AND SHOWING, BECAUSE THERE WEREN'T THAT MANY PEOPLE. I DIDN'T
KNOW THEM ALL, BUT AT LEAST I KNEW WHAT THEY WERE DOING, AND HAD SEEN
THEIR WORK PREVIOUSLY. OF COURSE, THAT IS NOT THE CASE AT ALL NOW. THE
NUMBER OF PEOPLE INVOLVED ON A CREATIVE OR SERIOUS LEVEL WITH PHOTOGRAPHY

IS STILL RELATIVELY SMALL. HOWEVER, IT IS CERTAINLY NOT AN "UNDERGROUND"
ACTIVITY WHEN YOU HAVE NEWSWEEK ARTICLES CONCERNED WITH PHOTOGRAPHY.

QUESTION # 5: DO YOU THINK PHOTOGRAPHY HAS BECOME "BIG BUSINESS?"

ANSWER: WELL, I DON'T THINK SO IN TERMS OF THE INDIVIDUALS IN IT. BUT,
CERTAINLY, THE INSTITUTIONS THAT ARE CONNECTED WITH IT, SUCH AS --
MUSEUMS, UNIVERSITIES AND SCHOOLS. ONE COULD CONCEIVE OF THAT BEING A
BIG BUSINESS. CERTAINLY, EDUCATION AND THE TEACHING JOBS PHOTOGRAPHY
HAS PROVIDED IN THE LAST TEN YEARS OR SO, ARE DUE TO THE BUSINESS TYPE
OF IDEA.

QUESTION # 6: HOW DO THE GALLERIES FOR PHOTOGRAPHY TODAY COMPARE WITH
               THE PHOTOGRAPHIC GALLERIES WHEN YOU FIRST BEGAN TO EXHIBIT?

ANSWER: WELL, OBVIOUSLY, THE NUMBER HAS INCREASED SIGNIFICANTLY, AND
THE LONGEVITY OF THE GALLERIES IS ALWAYS SORT OF TENTATIVE. I CAN RECALL
THAT HERE IN LOS ANGELES, AND OTHER PLACES, THERE WOULD BE GALLERIES THAT
WOULD BE OPEN FOUR MONTHS, FIVE MONTHS, SIX MONTHS, WITHOUT TAKING ANY
OBVIOUS PROFESSIONAL POSTURE. THEY WERE MORE LIKE STORE FRONTS.
     NOW, YOU HAVE GALLERIES LIKE THE LIGHT GALLERY, WHICH IS PROBABLY
ONE OF THE MOST SOPHISTICATED GALLERIES AROUND, AND IT IS PROFESSIONALLY
HANDLED. THERE IS ALSO THE FOCUS GALLERY, WHICH HAS ABOUT A FIFTEEN YEAR
HISTORY. SO THINGS HAVE CHANGED IN TERMS OF THE GALLERIES' CAPACITY TO
ENDURE.
     I STILL THINK THAT THERE ARE NOT A LOT OF SALES THROUGH THESE
GALLERIES. WHATEVER SALES THERE ARE, TEND TO GO HALF TO INSTITUTIONS AND
MUSEUM COLLECTIONS, RATHER THAN TO INDIVIDUALS WHO ARE VERY SERIOUSLY
INTERESTED IN CONTEMPORARY PHOTOGRAPHY. I DON'T KNOW IF MORE OF A MARKET
EXISTS NOW THAN THERE EVER WAS. OBVIOUSLY, IT HAS INCREASED SOMEWHAT.
     THERE IS THE IDEA FLOATING AROUND THAT PHOTOGRAPHS ARE HOT
ITEMS TO SELL. WELL, IT'S REALLY 19th CENTURY PHOTOGRAPHS WHICH ARE STILL
SELLING. THAT'S WHAT PEOPLE BUY MORE THAN CONTEMPORARY WORK. SO, THAT
HASN'T CHANGED A LOT.
     IT WILL BE INTERESTING TO SEE IF THERE WILL BE A REAL GENUINE
INTEREST IN SOCIETY FOR PHOTOGRAPHS, AS ART OBJECTS. IT WILL BE INTEREST-
ING TO SEE WHAT WILL HAPPEN WHEN ALL THE 19th CENTURY PHOTOGRAPHS ARE
GONE, WHICH WILL NOT BE TOO LONG FROM NOW.
     PEOPLE ARE STILL DIGGING UP PHOTOGRAPHS DATING FROM THE EARLY
PART OF THE CENTURY BY PHOTOGRAPHERS WHO WERE NOT REALLY THE MOST CREATIVE
OR MOST SIGNIFICANT. SIMPLY BECAUSE THE PEOPLE ARE DEAD OR FROM ANOTHER
ERA, THOSE PHOTOGRAPHS RETAIN A FLAVOR OF BEING RARE. I HOPE THAT WILL
CHANGE EVENTUALLY.
     RIGHT NOW, IF SOMEONE IS GOING TO START A COLLECTION OF PHOTO-
GRAPHS, THEY DON'T START OUT WITH CONTEMPORARY WORK. THEY GO BACK AND
PICK UP PEOPLE LIKE SISKIND, CALLAHAN, THAT SORT OF THING. THOSE PHOTO-
GRAPHS ARE MARKETABLE. I'M NOT SAYING THEY ARE NOT CONTEMPORARY, BUT,
THEY ARE CERTAINLY NOT PHOTOGRAPHS BY PEOPLE WHO ARE CHANGING THINGS AND
BRINGING NEW PICTURES AND IDEAS INTO THE SITUATION.

QUESTION # 7: IS THERE AN "ESTABLISHED" POINT OF VIEW VERSUS AN "AVANT-
               GARDE" POINT OF VIEW IN FINE ART PHOTOGRAPHY, AND IF YOU
               THINK THERE IS, PLEASE CHARACTERIZE IT?

ANSWER: THAT'S ALSO AN INTERESTING QUESTION. IN MY MEMORY, WHEN I FIRST BEGAN WORKING IN PHOTOGRAPHY, I CERTAINLY HAD THE ATTITUDE OR FEELING THAT THERE WAS AN "ESTABLISHED" POINT OF VIEW THAT I WAS WORKING AGAINST. I FELT THAT I WAS WORKING IN SOME ALTERNATIVE WAY.

I THINK THAT'S NOT SO COMMON AN IDEA TODAY. THE ATTITUDE IS LESS PREVALENT NOW THAT THERE IS A PARTICULAR WAY YOU HAVE TO PHOTOGRAPH OR A PARTICULAR KIND OF PHOTOGRAPH THAT IS ACCEPTABLE. IT IS MUCH MORE LIBERAL AS THE MEDIUM EXPANDS AND CONTINUES EXPANDING RAPIDLY.

IF THERE IS ANY "ESTABLISHED" POINT OF VIEW, IT CHANGES SO RAPIDLY, THAT IT IS HARD TO SEE WHAT IT IS. I THINK THAT THE INSTITUTIONS, AS THEY ALWAYS WERE, ARE CONSERVATIVE, AS OPPOSED TO LOOKING TO MORE AVANT-GARDE IDEAS. I THINK THAT FOR PHOTOGRAPHERS NOW, THERE IS MORE POTENTIAL FOR VISIBILITY AND GETTING THEIR WORK IN THE PUBLIC EYE. THEY SEEM TO BE MORE INVOLVED PROFESSIONALLY IN EXHIBITION POSSIBILITIES AND SALES, THAN I SENSE I WAS, IN THE BEGINNING. FOR ME, IT WAS MORE A MATTER OF A "DO IT AND SEE WHAT HAPPENS" ATTITUDE. TO SOME EXTENT, THIS ATTITUDE IS STILL PRESENT IN MY WORK TODAY.

I THINK PEOPLE HAVE MORE OF A FEELING THAT THERE IS A COMMUNITY; THERE IS A GROUP OF PEOPLE; THERE IS SOME INTEREST IN PHOTOGRAPHY. I THINK THAT HAS SHIFTED FOR THE BETTER.

QUESTION # 8:   SO, DO YOU FEEL, WHEN YOU BEGAN, THAT YOU WERE ATTEMPTING TO ESTABLISH A NEW POINT OF VIEW WHICH WAS BEING OPPOSED; WHEREAS, NOW THE IMAGERY IN PHOTOGRAPHY HAS BECOME MORE LIBERAL, AND AS A RESULT, PHOTOGRAPHERS WHO ARE CREATING WORK, WHICH IS NOT IN THE MAIN GENRE, CAN BE MORE EASILY ACCEPTED?

ANSWER: I THINK SO. I ALWAYS THINK ABOUT IT. IN FACT, IF YOU COULD TALK TO NATHAN LYONS ABOUT THIS, IT WOULD BE VERY INTERESTING. AT EASTMAN HOUSE IN THE MID-60's, HE DID TWO REALLY INTERESTING SHOWS. ONE WAS ENTITLED, "PERSISTENCE OF VISION." NOW THE PICTURES DO NOT LOOK ALL THAT AVANT-GARDE, BUT AT THE TIME THEY WERE QUITE DIFFERENT FROM WHAT WE WERE ACCUS-TOMED TO SEEING. THE OTHER SHOW WAS "TOWARDS A SOCIAL LANDSCAPE," WHICH INCLUDED ROBERT FRANK, FRIEDLANDER, WINOGRAND, DANNY LYONS AND OTHERS. BOTH OF THESE BOOKS AND EXHIBITS WERE RATHER WIDELY CIRCULATED.

I THINK THERE WAS AN EFFECT AND COMMUNICATION CONCERNING ALTER-NATIVE POINTS OF VIEW PRACTICED THROUGH THESE EXHIBITS AND BOOKS.

I DO NOT THINK WE HAVE THAT SITUATION, NOW. THE IDEA THAT YOU HAVE DEFINITIVE ALTERNATIVES DOES NOT EXIST AT THIS TIME. THE WORK EXHIBITED IN THESE SHOWS WAS CLEARLY ALTERNATIVE; WHEREAS, NOW THE ALTERNATIVES ARE LESS DEFINED!

HAROLD JONES

BORN SEPTEMBER 29, 1940
BEGAN PHOTOGRAPHY 1962

QUESTION # 1:   HOW DO YOU FEEL PHOTOGRAPHY, AS AN ART FORM, HAS CHANGED
DURING YOUR LIFE TIME?

ANSWER: THERE ARE MORE PEOPLE DOING IT NOW THAN WHEN I STARTED. THAT
IS ONE WAY THAT IT HAS CHANGED.

QUESTION # 2:   HOW DO YOU FEEL PHOTOGRAPHY HAS CHANGED FROM THE AESTHETIC
STANDPOINT?

ANSWER: THE VARIETY OF PEOPLE DOING PHOTOGRAPHY CERTAINLY MEANS MORE
IDEAS ARE BEING DEALT WITH THAN WHEN I STARTED PHOTOGRAPHY FIFTEEN
YEARS AGO. IT HAS BECOME A LOT MORE INTRICATE, COMPLEX AND INTERESTING.

QUESTION # 3:   DO YOU FEEL THE MOTIVATIONS OF YOUNG PHOTOGRAPHERS TODAY
DIFFER FROM YOUR ORIGINAL MOTIVATIONS AND CONCERNS WITH
PHOTOGRAPHY?

ANSWER: I AM SURE WHEN I STARTED THERE WERE VARIOUS MOTIVATIONS FOR PHOTO-
GRAPHERS. SO I WOULD IMAGINE THE MOTIVATIONS ARE AS VARIED NOW AS THEY
WERE WHEN I STARTED. I WOULD SAY THERE ARE MORE PEOPLE INVOLVED NOW, BUT
I WOULD THINK THAT THE MOTIVATIONS ARE PROBABLY THE SAME.

QUESTION # 4:   DO YOU FEEL THE INVOLVEMENT OF MORE PEOPLE IN PHOTOGRAPHY
IS TO THE ADVANTAGE OF PHOTOGRAPHY, OR DO YOU FEEL IT HAS
PUT A DAMPER ON CREATIVITY?

ANSWER: NO, I THINK IT IS AN IMPORTANT SIGN. THERE ARE MORE PAINTERS
NOW, MORE PRINTMAKERS, MORE CRAFTS PEOPLE. THERE ARE MORE PHOTOGRAPHERS,
MORE WRITERS. IT SEEMS AS IF THERE ARE MORE PEOPLE WHO HAVE TIME TO
DO THIS SORT OF THING.
        I THINK THE THING WHICH HAS NOT INCREASED IS THE AUDIENCE, WHICH
CAN BE A PROBLEM FOR ALL THE ARTISTS DOING THINGS. RIGHT NOW, THERE ARE
MORE GOOD PHOTOGRAPHERS THAN THERE ARE PLACES FOR THEM ALL TO SHOW OR TO
EXHIBIT THEIR WORK. WE DO NOT HAVE A SYSTEM TO ASSIMILATE ALL THE ARTISTS
INTO OUR CULTURE AND SUPPORT THEM ALL. IT IS A VERY HARD THING TO DO.

QUESTION # 5:   DO YOU THINK FINE ART PHOTOGRAPHY HAS BECOME A "BIG
BUSINESS?"

ANSWER: I DO NOT THINK IT HAS BECOME A BIG BUSINESS. I THINK IT HAS
BECOME A SUBSTANTIAL MINOR BUSINESS WITHIN THE ART WORLD.
        NEW YORK IS ALWAYS LOOKING FOR A "FAD" TO TURN OVER FOR MORE
MONEY. CERTAINLY, THERE ARE MORE PEOPLE MAKING A LIVING AT MAKING THEIR
OWN PHOTOGRAPHS THAN THERE WERE TEN OR FIFTEEN YEARS AGO.

QUESTION # 6:   HOW DO THE GALLERIES FOR PHOTOGRAPHY TODAY COMPARE WITH
THE PHOTOGRAPHIC GALLERIES WHEN YOU FIRST BEGAN YOUR
INVOLVEMENT WITH PHOTOGRAPHY?

ANSWER: WHEN I STARTED IN PHOTOGRAPHY, THERE WERE HARDLY ANY GALLERIES AT ALL. THERE WAS THE EXPOSURE GALLERY IN NEW YORK. IT WAS REALLY THE ONLY PHOTO GALLERY IN NEW YORK. I GUESS A COUPLE OF YEARS AFTER THAT THE WITKIN GALLERY OPENED UP.

QUESTION # 7: WERE YOU THERE DURING THE TIME OF THE UNDERGROUND GALLERY?

ANSWER: YES, I REMEMBER THE UNDERGROUND GALLERY, BUT I GOT THERE AFTER IT WAS OVER. THERE REALLY WERE NOT VERY MANY PLACES WE COULD GO. THE MOST IMPORTANT THINGS FOR US WERE BOOKS. WE WOULD ALL RUN OUT AND BUY THE LATEST BOOK THAT CAME OUT. PHOTOGRAPHIC BOOKS WERE SOMETHING WE WERE MORE AWARE OF. ALSO, WHEN I WAS IN GRADUATE SCHOOL, WE WERE MORE AWARE OF THE STUDENTS WHO WERE ENROLLED IN OTHER GRADUATE PROGRAMS. AN EXAMPLE WOULD BE, WHEN I WAS A STUDENT AT NEW MEXICO, WE KNEW WHO THE STUDENTS WERE IN HENRY HOLMES SMITH'S PROGRAM AND JACK WELPOTT'S PROGRAM IN CHICAGO. WE WERE ABLE TO TRADE A LOT OF INFORMATION, MORE THAN IS REALLY POSSIBLE NOW BECAUSE THERE ARE SO MANY PEOPLE DOING PHOTOGRAPHY.

QUESTION # 8: IF YOU HAVE EVER ATTEMPTED TO EXHIBIT IN A GALLERY, WHICH WAS NOT DEDICATED TO PHOTOGRAPHY (AN "ART GALLERY"), WHAT WAS THE RESPONSE?

ANSWER: I HAVE AN EXHIBIT DOWNTOWN IN AN "ART GALLERY" NOW. I AM MORE INTERESTED IN THE ART AUDIENCE THAN I AM IN THE PHOTOGRAPHIC AUDIENCE, BECAUSE OF THE KIND OF PICTURES I MAKE. THE PHOTO-GRAPHIC AUDIENCE, IN GENERAL, IS A VERY LIMITED AUDIENCE. GENERALLY, THE PHOTOGRAPHIC AUDIENCE IS VERY LIMITED IN THEIR KNOWLEDGE OF THE OTHER ART MEDIUMS OR CONCEPTS OF ART-- WHICH ARE ISSUES I ADDRESS IN MY WORK. SO I REALLY TRY NOT TO SHOW IN JUST STRAIGHT PHOTO GALLERIES, WHEN I CAN HELP IT.
I AM MUCH MORE INTERESTED IN THE RESPONSE FROM PEOPLE IN OTHER MEDIUMS, SUCH AS WRITER FRIENDS OF MINE, POETS AND PAINTERS. THESE PEOPLE'S RESPONSES ARE MUCH MORE INTERESTING AND IMPORTANT TO ME THAN GENERALLY, A PHOTOGRAPHIC AUDIENCE, WHICH I TEND TO FIND VERY NARROW MINDED, INTROVERTED AND INBRED.
THE PEOPLE WHO ARE MOST BORING TO TALK TO ABOUT PHOTOGRAPHY ARE PEOPLE WHO HAVE GONE TO PHOTOGRAPHY PROGRAMS AND THAT IS THE ONLY THING THEY HAVE EVER TALKED ABOUT -- NOT PAINTING, MUSIC OR ANY OTHER MEDIUM. I DO NOT LEARN ANYTHING TALKING TO THESE PEOPLE.

QUESTION # 9: DO YOU PERCEIVE AN INFLUX IN PHOTOGRAPHY, AND IF YOU DO, PLEASE CHARACTERIZE IT?

ANSWER: ONE OF THE THINGS I SEE NOW IS PHOTOGRAPHERS MAKING THEIR OWN IMAGERY. THE KINDS OF PICTURES THEY MAKE, AND THE ISSUES THEY ARE CONCERNED WITH REALLY RELATE TO ISSUES WHICH ARE TRADITIONALLY OUTSIDE THE AREA OF PHOTOGRAPHY, SUCH AS -- ANTHROPOLOGY, SOCIOLOGY, AND CULTURAL OBSERVATIONS, WHICH I FIND VERY INTERESTING.
I THINK THERE IS A CROSS-POLLINATION OF IDEAS. I AM VERY INTERESTED IN THAT. I SEE PHOTOGRAPHERS INGESTING OTHER IDEAS FROM OUT-SIDE, SO THEIR WORK BECOMES MORE VARIED IN ITS APPROACH. ANOTHER THING WHICH IS HAPPENING TODAY IS THAT BECAUSE THERE ARE SO MANY VARIOUS APPROACHES TO MAKING PHOTOGRAPHS, IT BECOMES VERY EXCITING.
WHEN I BEGAN, THE PEOPLE WE REALLY LOOKED TO WERE PEOPLE I GUESS WE WOULD CALL "ART PHOTOGRAPHERS," QUOTE, UNQUOTE. TODAY, THERE ARE SO MANY REALLY RICH IDEAS WHICH PEOPLE ARE DEALING WITH. YOU COULD GO

FROM A BOOK LIKE EVIDENCE, WHICH IS ONE END OF THE SCALE TO BELLOCQ'S
PICTURES, WHICH LEE FRIEDLANDER FOUND. I THINK THAT OPENS A SPECTRUM
WHICH IS JUST FABULOUS. I THINK IT IS GOING TO KEEP EXPANDING, EXPLOD-
ING AND UNFOLDING INTO OTHER AREAS.

QUESTION # 10:   DO YOU FEEL THAT FINE ART PHOTOGRAPHY, WHEN YOU BEGAN,
                  WAS AN "UNDERGROUND" ACTIVITY, WITH ONLY A FEW PEOPLE
                  INVOLVED?

ANSWER: I GUESS WE ALWAYS THOUGHT THAT. I CAN REMEMBER BEING AT EASTMAN
HOUSE, WHICH IS WHERE I WENT AFTER I GOT OUT OF GRADUATE SCHOOL. WE
WERE DEDICATED AND WE ALWAYS WISHED MORE PEOPLE WERE INTERESTED. I CAN
REMEMBER HAVING CONVERSATIONS. WE WERE ALWAYS BITCHING, "WHY WERE THERE
NOT MORE PEOPLE INTERESTED IN PHOTOGRAPHY?" THIS WAS ONLY TEN YEARS AGO.
I GUESS WE WERE MORE EFFECTIVE THAN WE THOUGHT. I CAN REMEMBER THOSE
CONVERSATIONS.
        I CAN REMEMBER WHEN CALLAHAN PRINTS WERE $25.00.
        EVERY TIME A NEW PHOTOGRAPHIC BOOK CAME OUT, WE WOULD RUN AND GET
IT TO SEE WHAT IT WAS. A MAJOR PHOTOGRAPHIC EXHIBIT, ANYWHERE IN THE
COUNTRY, WAS A BIG DEAL. YES, I CAN REMEMBER ALL THAT.

QUESTION # 11:   IS THERE AN "ESTABLISHED" POINT OF VIEW VERSUS AN
                  AVANT-GARDE" POINT OF VIEW IN FINE ART PHOTOGRAPHY,
                  AND IF YOU THINK THERE IS, PLEASE CHARACTERIZE IT?

ANSWER: I THINK THERE ARE PEOPLE WHO DELUDE THEMSELVES BY IMAGINING
THEY HAVE THE AVANT-GARDE OR "THE POINT OF VIEW" IN PHOTOGRAPHY. THERE
IS A CIRCLE OF "SYCOPHANTS," FOR INSTANCE, AROUND JOHN SZARKOWSKI, WHO
BELIEVE HE HAS "THE WAY" OF MAKING PHOTOGRAPHS, PERIOD, "THE WAY,"
CAPITAL, "THE WAY."
        IT FASCINATES ME AND IT IS REALLY UNFORTUNATE THAT THESE PEOPLE
FEEL THIS WAY, BUT, I ADMIRE THE "LUXURY" THAT THEY KNOW ABSOLUTELY WHAT
PHOTOGRAPHY IS. I DO NOT HAVE THAT "LUXURY."
        I AM INTERESTED IN HOW MANY DIFFERENT PHOTOGRAPHERS ARE WORKING
IN HOW MANY DIFFERENT WAYS. I THINK IT IS REMARKABLE THERE ARE PEOPLE
WHO FEEL THEY ARE ON THE EDGE OF THE AVANT-GARDE.
        THERE ARE SO MANY PEOPLE WORKING WITH SO MANY DIFFERENT AND
VARIED IDEAS. WE HAVE ATMOSPHERIC PHYSICISTS HERE MAKING PHOTOGRAPHS
OF THE THINGS THAT HAPPEN IN THE SKY, WHICH ARE JUST REMARKABLE! MEDICAL
ILLUSTRATION PHOTOGRAPHY IS NOW BEING MADE, WHICH IS JUST BEAUTIFUL! I
RECENTLY HAD THE PLEASURE OF SEEING THE PHOTOGRAPHS THE APOLLO ASTRONAUTS
MADE ON THE MOON, ALL OF THEM -- THEY ARE AMAZING!
        I AM INTERESTED, AS A PHOTOGRAPHER. I FEED OFF OF AND RESPOND
TO THE THINGS WHICH ARE HAPPENING. THERE IS REALLY SO MUCH TO DEAL WITH,
THAT I FIND IT EXCITING! I LIKE IT!
        I KNOW THERE ARE PEOPLE WHO THINK THEY HAVE THE AVANT-GARDE IN
PHOTOGRAPHY. I THINK IT IS HILARIOUS THAT THEY THINK SUCH A THING. I
AM MUCH MORE INTERESTED IN THINGS WHICH OCCUR IN AREAS I NEVER IMAGINED
BEFORE.

QUESTION # 12:   I AM FINISHED WITH THE FORMAL QUESTIONS AT THIS POINT,
                  SO I WOULD LIKE TO ASK YOU IF YOU HAVE ANYTHING ELSE
                  YOU WOULD LIKE TO ADD, AT THIS TIME?

ANSWER: I THINK THE CULTURE HAS CHANGED IN THE LAST FIFTEEN YEARS. AN EXAMPLE WOULD BE THAT WHEN I STARTED THE LIGHT GALLERY IN NEW YORK IN 1971, IT WAS INTERESTING TO NOTE WHAT EXHIBITS WITKIN WAS SHOWING UP TO THAT POINT, AND HOW ALL THAT CHANGED IN NEW YORK.

I WOULD SHOW WORK PEOPLE DID EVERY TWO YEARS, OUT OF THE FLOW OF THEIR WORK, BECAUSE THE PEOPLE I KNEW WERE ALWAYS WORKING ALL THE TIME. THIS WOULD ABSOLUTELY FLOOR PEOPLE IN NEW YORK BECAUSE THEY THOUGHT PHOTO-GRAPHERS WORKED TO HAVE BOOKS PUBLISHED. SO MUCH HAS CHANGED IN ALL THE TIME FROM THAT POINT. IT IS REALLY VERY COMPLICATED AND VERY WONDERFUL!

QUESTION # 13: I AM INTERESTED IN YOUR HISTORY WITH THE LIGHT GALLERY, THE CENTER FOR CREATIVE PHOTOGRAPHY, AND NOW, YOUR INVOLVEMENT WITH THE COORDINATION OF THE PHOTOGRAPHY DEPARTMENT AT THE UNIVERSITY OF ARIZONA. WHAT WERE YOUR MOTIVATIONS FOR CHANGING FROM ONE POSITION TO ANOTHER?

ANSWER: I COULD PRETTY MUCH GUARANTEE YOU THAT WHAT I AM DOING NOW WILL BE THE JOB I WILL HAVE UNTIL I RETIRE. I ENJOY TEACHING.

LET US BACK UP. THE OPPORTUNITY TO GO TO NEW YORK WAS A FLUKE. I CAME FROM THE EASTMAN HOUSE, FROM THE POSITION OF ASSISTANT CURATOR. I WAS THERE WHEN NATHAN LYONS LEFT, AND I STAYED A YEAR AFTER HE LEFT. I STAYED A YEAR AFTER NATHAN BECAUSE I FELT RESPONSIBLE FOR SOME OF THE IDEAS HE STARTED, AND I STAYED TO KEEP THEM GOING. I WAS GOING TO LEAVE TO GO TO U.C.L.A. TO TEACH, AND THIS GUY CALLED ME FROM NEW YORK TO START THIS GALLERY OF LARGE COLOR SAIL BOAT PICTURES, WHICH WAS EXACTLY WHAT I DID NOT WANT TO DO.

QUESTION # 14: SO HE WANTED YOU TO START A COMMERCIAL GALLERY?

ANSWER: YES, HE DID. I WAS TERRIFIED OF NEW YORK, NUMBER ONE, AND NUMBER TWO, I WAS NOT SURE THAT I WAS A BUSINESSMAN AT THE TIME. IT WAS A TERRIFYING DECISION. I FINALLY DECIDED TO TRY IT FOR A YEAR. I ENDED STAYING FOR FIVE YEARS. I WAS VERY INTERESTED IN TRYING TO DEVELOP AN AUDIENCE FOR PHOTOGRAPHY -- THAT IS HOW I LOOKED AT WHAT I WAS DOING. ONE OF MY BUSINESS FRIEND'S COMMENTS ABOUT LIGHT GALLERY WAS, "IT COULD NOT MAKE UP ITS MIND IF IT WAS AN EDUCATIONAL ENTERPRISE OR A BUSINESS ENTERPRISE." WELL, OF COURSE, IT WAS BOTH.

I BEGAN TO REALIZE HOW DECISIONS WERE MADE IN THE NEW YORK ART WORLD. IT BECAME VERY CLEAR TO ME THAT IT HAD VERY LITTLE TO DO WITH THE ACTUAL VALUE OF THE WORK. MOST OF THE DECISIONS WERE POLITICALLY RELATED TO HOW MUCH SOMEONE LIKED THE PHOTOGRAPHER. IF THE PHOTOGRAPHER HAD ENOUGH MONEY TO CONTRIBUTE ON HIS OWN, SO IT WAS NOT COSTING THE MUSEUM OR GALLERY ANY MONEY -- IF THE PHOTOGRAPHER WAS GOING TO PUT OUT A BOOK -- THE GALLERY WOULD BE CRAZY TO TURN DOWN THE WORK, AND SO ON, AND SO FORTH. IT WAS INTERESTING. I THINK EVERY STUDENT SHOULD HAVE A COURSE IN THE PRACTICAL POLITICS OF THE ART WORLD.

IT BECAME A SOURCE OF GREAT CONCERN TO ME THAT A LOT OF THE DECISIONS WERE MADE, NOT ABOUT THE WORK, BUT, RATHER ABOUT OTHER THINGS. THE GENERAL AUDIENCE WAS CONSIDERING THE DECISIONS TO BE DIRECTLY RELATED TO THE WORK, WHICH WAS NOT TRUE, IF YOU WATCHED HOW DECISIONS WERE MADE. OCCASIONALLY, AN EXHIBIT OR BOOK WOULD BE REALLY ABOUT THE MERITS OF THE WORK. BUT, I FOUND THAT TO BE AN EXCEPTION TO THE RULE.

QUESTION # 15:   DO YOU FEEL, THEN, THAT THE POLITICS WERE MORE OF A
                 DECIDING FACTOR IN TERMS OF WHO GOT WHAT EXHIBIT, RATHER
                 THAN BEING BASED ON THE ACTUAL AESTHETIC VALUE OF THE ART
                 WORKS?

ANSWER: ABSOLUTELY, ABSOLUTELY, YES!

         WHAT I AM DOING NOW IS A COMPLETELY DIFFERENT EXPERIENCE, WITH
THE INCREDIBLE COLLECTION AT THE CENTER FOR CREATIVE PHOTOGRAPHY, WHICH
IS DESIGNED FOR STUDENTS. I NOW HAVE THE OPPORTUNITY TO TEACH, BECAUSE
I FEEL THAT I HAVE INFORMATION WHICH STUDENTS CAN USE. I AM WORKING NOW
TO DEVELOP AN AUDIENCE, AS WELL AS, PHOTOGRAPHERS.

DAVID HOWARD

BORN 1948
STARTED PHOTOGRAPHY 1967

QUESTION # 1:   HOW DO YOU FEEL PHOTOGRAPHY, AS AN ART FORM, HAS
                CHANGED IN YOUR LIFE TIME?

ANSWER: I FEEL THAT THE STYLES WHICH HAVE DEVELOPED IN PHOTOGRAPHY
HAVE BECOME MORE LIBERAL.
        WHEN I BEGAN PHOTOGRAPHY SERIOUSLY, APPROXIMATELY TEN YEARS
AGO, PHOTOGRAPHY WAS MORE STRINGENTLY CONCEIVED IN RELATION TO ITS
OVERALL AESTHETIC PERSUASIONS. DIVERGENT PHILOSOPHIC PERSUASIONS WERE
FROWNED UPON.
        SOME PHOTOGRAPHERS COULD BE CONSIDERED AVANT-GARDE AT THE TIME.
THEY BROKE THE GROUND FOR MORE LIBERALIZED TYPES OF IMAGERY. PRIOR TO
THESE PHOTOGRAPHERS, WHO WERE BREAKING SOME OF THE TRADITIONS WHICH
HAD BEEN ESTABLISHED, PHOTOGRAPHY WAS DEALING PRIMARILY WITH A VISUAL
ORIENTATION. AS TIME WENT ON, PHOTOGRAPHY BECAME MORE AND MORE LIBERATED.
THE PHOTOGRAPHERS REALIZED THEY COULD DO ANYTHING WITH PHOTOGRAPHY.
PHOTOGRAPHY FINALLY BEGAN TAKING A GIANT STEP IN DIRECTIONS OTHER THAN
THE PHOTOGRAPHIC PRINT. SEQUENTIAL FORMATS BUILT UP, PHOTOGRAPHIC SCULP-
TURE WAS BEING MADE, AND VARIOUS UNCONVENTIONAL PRINTING TECHNIQUES WERE
BEING MORE WIDELY CIRCULATED. THE SILVER PRINT WAS NO LONGER THE ONLY
OUTLET FOR PHOTOGRAPHERS. PHOTOGRAPHY WAS BEING USED AS AN INTEGRAL PART
IN "AESTHETIC EVENTS," AND CONCEPTUAL ART, TO THE POINT THAT, THERE WAS
NO DIFFERENTIATION BETWEEN THE PHOTOGRAPHS AND THE ACTUAL EVENTS OR CON-
CEPTS. THEY BECAME ONE AND THE SAME. PRIOR TO THIS, PHOTOGRAPHY WAS
STRICTLY COMING FROM THE STANDPOINT OF WHAT WE WOULD CALL THE "IMAGE."
THE IMAGE AS AN OBJECT-ORIENTED PIECE WAS IMPORTANT, AND THE EMOTIONAL
EFFECT OF THE IMAGE WAS THE MAIN IDEA.
        PHOTOGRAPHS WHICH WERE DEPICTING REALITY WERE THE MAIN THRUST
OF SOME OF THE FIRST PHOTOGRAPHIC TRENDS; WHEREAS, THE "IMAGE," PHOTOGRAPH-
IC SCULPTURE AND CONCEPTUAL PHOTOGRAPHS WERE MORE SUBJECTIVE, AND EVOLVED
LATER ON.

QUESTION # 2:   DO YOU FEEL THE MOTIVATIONS OF YOUNG PHOTOGRAPHERS TODAY
                DIFFER FROM YOUR ORIGINAL MOTIVATIONS AND CONCERNS WITH
                PHOTOGRAPHY?

ANSWER: I WOULD CONSIDER MYSELF TO BE ONE OF THE YOUNG PHOTOGRAPHERS
TO BEGIN WITH, SO IT IS A LITTLE DIFFICULT FOR ME TO PERCEIVE WHAT
PEOPLE YOUNGER THAN MYSELF ARE DOING. HOWEVER, I DO THINK THE PEOPLE
WHO ARE YOUNGER THAN MYSELF WHO ARE BEGINNING PHOTOGRAPHY, ARE BECOMING
EVEN MORE RADICAL.
        WHEN I BEGAN PHOTOGRAPHY, MY ART WORK, I THINK, WAS CONSIDERED
RADICAL. WHEN I BEGAN GOING INTO PHOTOGRAPHIC CONSTRUCTION, CUTTING
OUT PHOTOGRAPHS CIRCULARLY AND MOUNTING THEM ON RELIEF, AND PUTTING THEM
INTO GEOMETRIC PATTERNS WITH SERIES -- THAT WAS AVANT-GARDE. BUT, AS
TIME GOES ON, IT BECOMES LESS AND LESS AVANT-GARDE. NOW, PEOPLE ARE
DOING THINGS THAT ARE EVEN MORE RADICAL.
        THE TECHNICAL CONCERNS ARE LESS STRESSED RECENTLY. I WAS
INVOLVED WITH THE IDEA THAT THE PHOTOGRAPH SHOULD BE A FINE PRINT. IT
WAS A TRADITION. AS TIME GOES ON, THIS IS STRESSED LESS AND LESS. THE
IMAGE BECAME THE MOST IMPORTANT ASPECT. PHOTOGRAPHERS ARE REALIZING THAT
A PHOTOGRAPH WHICH IS PRINTED WELL AND IS DEVOID OF EMOTIONAL IMPACT,
IS DEAD; WHEREAS, A PHOTOGRAPH WHICH HAS A GREAT EMOTIONAL EFFECT ON
THE VIEWER, BUT MAY NOT BE PRINTED VERY WELL, IS MUCH MORE REWARDING TO
THE VIEWER AND THE CREATOR OF THE PICTURE.

QUESTION # 3:   DO YOU THINK FINE ART PHOTOGRAPHY HAS BECOME "BIG
                BUSINESS?"

ANSWER: WELL, I THINK IT HAS BECOME A BUSINESS, MAYBE NOT A BIG
BUSINESS. SOME PHOTOGRAPHERS ARE OUT THERE HUSTLING AND MANIPULATING
THE PHOTOGRAPHY ART WORLD, AS IF IT WERE A REGULAR OUTLET OR BUSINESS
IN ANY OTHER AREA OF OUR SOCIETY. THERE ARE OTHER PHOTOGRAPHIC ARTISTS
WHO DO NOT APPROACH IT FROM A BUSINESS ASPECT, BUT RATHER CONCERN THEM-
SELVES PRIMARILY WITH THE EVOLUTION OF THEIR PHOTOGRAPHS. THEY HAVE NO
REAL BUSINESS INTENTIONS. SOME OTHER ARTISTS ARE OUT THERE WORKING MORE
ON GETTING AN INCOME FROM THEIR PHOTOGRAPHS AS ART WORK, MORE THAN THEY
ARE INVOLVED IN THE CREATION OF THEIR PHOTOGRAPHS.
        SO, IT BECOMES A BUSINESS, BUT IT DOES NOT BECOME A BIG BUSINESS,
BECAUSE IT IS NOT LUCRATIVE, BUT THEY CAN GET THEMSELVES INVOLVED WITH
WORKSHOPS, STATE AND FEDERAL GRANTS, GRANTS FROM PRIVATE INSTITUTIONS,
AND MORE. THIS CAN AMOUNT TO THOUSANDS AND THOUSANDS OF DOLLARS OF
REVENUE FOR ONE INDIVIDUAL. SO IT CAN BECOME A BUSINESS IN THAT RESPECT.
        SOME PHOTOGRAPHERS ARE APPROACHING IT FROM THAT STANDPOINT,
BUT I FEEL THAT THE MAJORITY ARE NOT. THERE IS OCCASIONALLY CURATORIAL
NEGLIGENCE, AND AS A RESULT, SOME PHOTOGRAPHERS CAN MAKE A BUSINESS OUT
OF IT. OTHER ARTISTS AND PHOTOGRAPHERS WHO ARE NOT OUT THERE AS BUSI-
NESSMEN, DO NOT GET AS MUCH RETURN BECAUSE THEY ARE NOT OUT THERE PUSHING.
        SOME PHOTOGRAPHERS HAVE BEEN AROUND FOR DECADES NOT TAKING THE
BUSINESSMAN APPROACH, WHO HAVE TO GO BEGGING BECAUSE THEY ARE NOT OUT
THERE AS BUSINESSMEN. OTHER YOUNG PHOTOGRAPHERS, AS PHOTOGRAPHY BECOMES
MORE POPULAR AND THE AUDIENCE GROWS LARGER, ARE WORKING FROM THE BUSINESS-
MAN APPROACH. THE OLDER PHOTOGRAPHERS, WHEN THEY BEGAN, HAD NO OUTLETS,
SO THEY ARE NOT GEARED-UP FOR A BUSINESS -- WHEREAS, THE YOUNGER PHOTO-
GRAPHERS STARTING OUT HAVE A LARGER OUTLET. THEY ARE TRYING TO INVOLVE
THEMSELVES AS MUCH AS POSSIBLE IN HOPES OF GETTING AN ECONOMIC RETURN.
OTHER PHOTOGRAPHERS THAT HAVE BEEN AROUND FOR TEN, TWENTY, THIRTY YEARS,
WHO ARE NOT OUT THERE HUSTLING, ARE NOT GETTING AS MUCH ECONOMIC SUPPORT.
THEY ARE COMING FROM AN AESTHETIC STANDPOINT, AND WHATEVER HAPPENS IN
RELATION TO THAT IS JUST TOPPING ON THE CAKE. THEY ARE MOSTLY CONCERNED
WITH THEIR PHOTOGRAPHS.

QUESTION # 4:   HOW DO THE GALLERIES FOR PHOTOGRAPHY TODAY COMPARE
                WITH THE PHOTOGRAPHIC GALLERIES WHEN YOU FIRST BEGAN
                TO EXHIBIT?

ANSWER: NOW THERE ARE MORE PHOTO GALLERIES, MOST DEFINITELY. I'D SAY
THAT THE GALLERIES HAVE MULTIPLIED IN THE LAST DECADE AT LEAST FIVE TO
TEN TIMES. WHEN I BEGAN, THERE WAS ONLY ONE PHOTOGRAPHIC GALLERY IN
NEW YORK, THE WITKIN, AND THERE WAS ONLY ONE PHOTOGRAPHIC GALLERY IN
SAN FRANCISCO, AND THAT WAS THE FOCUS. I BELIEVE THERE WEREN'T ANY
OTHER ESTABLISHED PHOTOGRAPHIC GALLERIES; AT THAT TIME, TO MY KNOWLEDGE,
THERE WERE ONLY A FEW GALLERIES. NOW IT SEEMS THERE ARE PHOTO GALLERIES
EVERYWHERE. MOST CITIES HAVE ABOUT THREE OR FOUR PHOTO GALLERIES, AND
SOME EVEN HAVE IN EXCESS OF TEN GALLERIES DEDICATED TO PHOTOGRAPHY IN
ONE CITY, LIKE NEW YORK -- RATHER THAN JUST ONE ON THE EAST COAST AND ONE
ON THE WEST COAST, LIKE IT USED TO BE. GALLERIES ARE NOW EXHIBITING
PHOTOGRAPHS QUITE FREQUENTLY, AS WELL. SO PHOTOGRAPHY GALLERIES HAVE
REALLY MULTIPLIED.

QUESTION # 5:   IF YOU HAVE EVER ATTEMPTED TO EXHIBIT IN A GALLERY, WHICH
                WAS NOT DEDICATED TO PHOTOGRAPHY (AN "ART GALLERY"), WHAT
                WAS THE RESPONSE?

ANSWER: WHEN I FIRST BEGAN TO EXHIBIT ABOUT EIGHT YEARS AGO, ART GALLER-
IES ALMOST COMPLETELY REJECTED THE IDEA OF EXHIBITING PHOTOGRAPHS. THEY
WOULDN'T DEAL WITH PHOTOGRAPHY AT ALL, AS FAR AS I'M CONCERNED, BECAUSE
IT WASN'T ECONOMICALLY FEASIBLE, FOR THEM.
          PHOTOGRAPHY WAS SELLING FOR ABOUT ONE HUNDRED DOLLARS A PRINT
AVERAGE BY A MASTER. THEY COULD SELL A **PAINTING** BY AN UNKNOWN FOR A
THOUSAND DOLLARS. A KNOWN ARTIST COULD SELL A PAINTING FOR AT LEAST
FIVE OR TEN THOUSAND DOLLARS, HANDS DOWN. SO TO SELL A PHOTOGRAPH FOR
A HUNDRED DOLLARS, BY A WELL-KNOWN PHOTOGRAPHER WAS ECONOMICALLY UNSOUND
FOR THESE GALLERIES. AS A RESULT, THEY WEREN'T WILLING TO DEAL WITH PHOTO-
GRAPHS. WHEN THE RECESSION SET IN, IN THE SEVENTIES, PEOPLE WEREN'T
AS INTERESTED IN BUYING PAINTINGS AT SUCH HIGH PRICES. THEY THEN STARTED
TO PURCHASE PHOTOGRAPHS. MOST OF THE ART GALLERIES I GOT INVOLVED WITH
WERE TOTALLY AGAINST EXHIBITING PHOTOGRAPHS, BUT I HAVE EXHIBITED PHOTO-
GRAPHS IN ART GALLERIES QUITE FREQUENTLY IN THE LAST THREE YEARS, AND IT
IS BECOMING MORE COMMON FOR ART GALLERIES TO EXHIBIT PHOTOGRAPHS. NOW
SOME ART GALLERIES ARE TURNING INTO PHOTOGRAPHIC GALLERIES AND THEY ARE
DISBANDING THEIR NORMAL PAINTING AND SCULPTURE EXHIBITIONS.

QUESTION # 6:   DO YOU PERCEIVE AN INFLUX IN PHOTOGRAPHY, AND IF YOU DO,
                PLEASE CHARACTERIZE IT?

ANSWER: THE FIRST QUESTION I ANSWERED AND SOME OF THE OTHER QUESTIONS
I THINK, HAVE ANSWERED THIS PARTICULAR QUESTION. THE ANSWER, IN ANY
EVENT, IS UNDOUBTEDLY, "YES." THERE IS A HUGE INFLUX IN PHOTOGRAPHY IN
RELATION TO THE AMOUNT OF PHOTOGRAPHERS WHO ARE NOW ATTEMPTING TO PRO-
DUCE PHOTOGRAPHIC ART WORKS; AND THE INFLUX, I THINK, IS ASTRONOMICAL,
AND I DON'T THINK IT HAS REACHED ITS CLIMAX YET!

QUESTION # 7:   DO YOU FEEL FINE ART PHOTOGRAPHY, WHEN YOU BEGAN, WAS AN
                "UNDERGROUND" ACTIVITY, WITH ONLY A FEW PEOPLE INVOLVED?

ANSWER: I DON'T THINK WHEN I BEGAN IT WAS AN "UNDERGROUND" ACTIVITY
NECESSARILY, BUT I DO FEEL THERE WERE A LOT FEWER PEOPLE INVOLVED, THAN
AT THE PRESENT TIME. PHOTOGRAPHY IS BECOMING MUCH MORE DISSEMINATED,
MUCH MORE WIDELY SPREAD. YOU CANNOT KEEP TRACK OF ALL THE DIFFERENT
PHOTOGRAPHIC ARTISTS AND WORKERS WHO ARE PRODUCING WORK NOW, BECAUSE
THERE IS SUCH A VAST AMOUNT OF PEOPLE INVOLVED. THE GALLERIES HAVE EX-
PANDED SO MUCH, IT'S ALMOST IMPOSSIBLE TO KEEP TRACK OF WHO IS DOING
WHAT. PRIOR TO THIS, IT WAS VERY EASY TO KEEP TRACK OF THE GALLERIES
AND WHO WAS EXHIBITING. NOW, IT'S VIRTUALLY IMPOSSIBLE.

QUESTION # 8:   IS THERE AN "ESTABLISHED" POINT OF VIEW VERSUS AN "AVANT-
                GARDE" POINT OF VIEW IN FINE ART PHOTOGRAPHY, AND IF THERE
                IS, COULD YOU PLEASE CHARACTERIZE IT?

ANSWER: WHEN I FIRST BEGAN, THERE WERE VARIOUS AVANT-GARDE TRENDS. I
DO FEEL AS IF THERE ARE VARIOUS AVANT-GARDE TRENDS OCCURRING NOW, AS WELL.
          THE AVANT-GARDE IS SIMPLY THE NEWEST THING TO COME ALONG, WHOSE
ACCEPTANCE IS QUESTIONABLE TO THE OVERALL TRADITIONS WHICH HAVE ALREADY
BEEN ACCEPTED BY THE PHOTOGRAPHIC COMMUNITY AT LARGE.
          THERE IS MORE THAN ONE PARTICULAR ESTABLISHED PHOTOGRAPHIC
PERSUASION. THERE ARE VARIOUS ESTABLISHED PHOTOGRAPHIC STYLES. AS ONE

PHOTOGRAPHIC ARTIST WILL COME ALONG AND ESTABLISH HIS OR HER WORK
THROUGH NATIONAL EXHIBITIONS, INTERNATIONAL EXHIBITIONS AND INTERNATIONAL
PUBLICATIONS -- THAT PHOTOGRAPHIC ARTIST BECOMES A HOUSEHOLD WORD IN
THE PHOTOGRAPHIC COMMUNITY. THAT IS WHAT I WOULD CALL THE "ESTABLISHED"
POINT OF VIEW.

        THE AVANT-GARDE IS SOMETHING WHICH HAS THE BEGINNINGS OF BEING
ESTABLISHED OR THE BEGINNINGS OF BEING REJECTED. THE CHARACTERIZATION
OF THE AVANT-GARDE, AT THIS POINT FOR ME, WOULD BE CONCEPTUAL PHOTOGRAPHY
AND CONCEPTUAL ART. THERE IS NO REAL DIVISION AT TIMES; THEY OVERLAP
SO MUCH. CONCEPTUALISM IS NOW ALMOST ACCEPTED AND SOON IT WILL NOT BE
AVANT-GARDE. COLOR PHOTOGRAPHY IS BECOMING EXTREMELY POPULAR, AND FOR
A WHILE, IT MAY HAVE BEEN CONSIDERED AVANT-GARDE. NOW IT IS BEING
CO-OPTED, AND IT IS BECOMING ESTABLISHED. ORIGINALLY, COLOR PHOTOGRAPHY
WAS ALMOST TOTALLY DISASSOCIATED FROM PHOTOGRAPHY AS AN ART FORM.

PERSPECTIVES

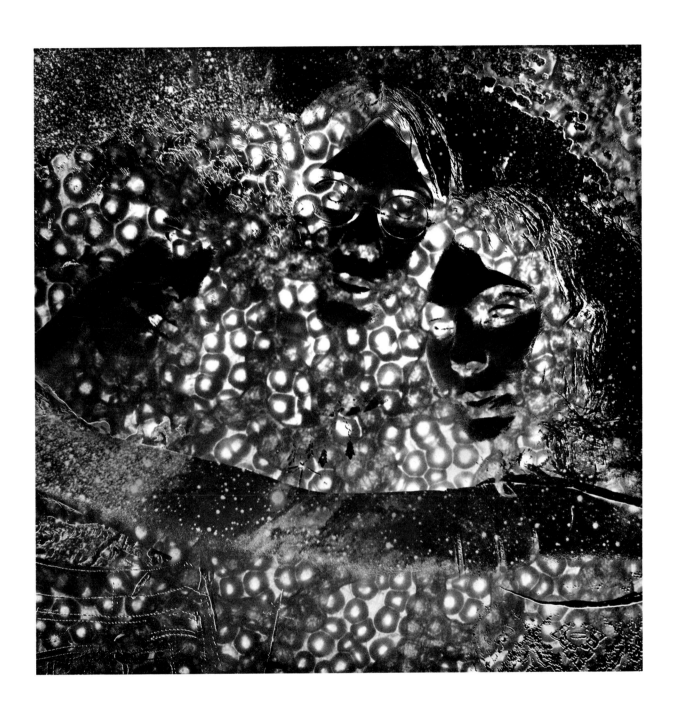

Each reality, each level of co_____ ____usness can overlap and the result ___ __mplete change of realty". When ___ vastly diff_rent levels of consc_ ___ overlap the result is a complete ___. The overlapping of ment_____ ____ either in the "min__ eye" ___ before __e ___di_____, __ _l eme__ge to ___ c___sciou_ ___the__ to be_ exa_mine_